D0477522

LGBT Matters

Matt Anniss

raintree
a Capstone company — publishers for children

Raintree is an imprint of Capstone Global Library Limited, a company incorporated in England and Wales having its registered office at 264 Banbury Road, Oxford, OX2 7DY – Registered company number: 6695582

www.raintree.co.uk
myorders@raintree.co.uk

Edited by Helen Cox Cannons
Designed by Dynamo Limited
Original illustrations © Capstone Global Library Limited 2019
Picture research by Dynamo Limited
Production by Katie LaVigne
Originated by Capstone Global Library Limited
Printed and bound in India

ISBN 978 1 4747 7296 9
22 21 20 19 18
10 9 8 7 6 5 4 3 2 1

British Library Cataloguing in Publication Data
A full catalogue record for this book is available from the British Library.

Acknowledgements
We would like to thank our consultant, Fiona Blee, for her invaluable help in the preparation of this book. We would also like to give warm thanks to all those who have contributed to this book.

We would like to thank the following for permission to reproduce photographs: Alamy: Custom Life Science Images, 8, dpa picture alliance, 12, dpa/Florian Schuh, 27 Top, Linda Dawn Hammond, 26, Maskot, Cover; Carys Jones-McNeill, 9; Georgia Barton-Hague, 21; Getty Images: iStock/DGLimages, 29, E+/joakimbkk, 22, iStock/olesiabilkei, 14, iStock/SolStock, 18, iStock/SoumenNath, 10, iStock/stevanovicigor, 23, iStock/studio-laska, 4, iStock/Vergani_Fotografia, 6, iStock/Wavebreakmedia, 20, WireImage/Debra L Rothenberg, 7, WireImage/Mike Marsland, 11, DigitalVision/Hinterhaus Productions, 16; Kelly Roskell-Thomas/www.instagram.com/amelias2mummies, 17; Max, 25; Newscom: AdMedia/Birdie Thompson, 24 left,PacificCoastNews/Jerry Perez, 24 Right, Splash News/Solent News, 27 Bottom; Owen Reading, 15; Rex/Shutterstock, 19; Shutterstock/A M Syed, 28.

Every effort has been made to contact copyright holders of material reproduced in this book. Any omissions will be rectified in subsequent printings if notice is given to the publisher.

All the internet addresses (URLs) given in this book were valid at the time of going to press. However, due to the dynamic nature of the internet, some addresses may have changed, or sites may have changed or ceased to exist since publication. While the author and publisher regret any inconvenience this may cause readers, no responsibility for any such changes can be accepted by either the author or the publisher.

Contents

Some words in this book appear in bold, **like this**.
You can find out what they mean by looking in the glossary.

What is LGBT?

When it comes to the heart, you cannot control which people you find attractive and fall in love with. Lots of men and women love each other very much. There are also men who love men, women who love women, and people who love both men and women. There are also men who feel more comfortable living their lives as women. And, of course, the other way round. Many of these people would say that they are part of the "LGBT community".

LGBT is a collective term that refers to four different types of people:

• **L**esbian

These are girls and women who are attracted to and have relationships with other girls and women.

• **G**ay

Boys and men who are attracted to and have relationships with other boys and men.

• **B**isexual

People who are attracted to both men and women and have relationships with either.

• **T**ransgender

The word "gender" is about whether someone is boy or girl, man or woman. Transgender people live their lives as a different gender from the one they were given at birth. For example, someone born into a male body may live their life as a woman. This is usually because that is how they feel inside.

This book looks at LGBT love, relationships and families, and the differing attitudes towards the community around the world. You can also find out about what it is like to be **lesbian**, **gay**, **bisexual** or transgender in the 21st century.

Changing attitudes

Big street parties in support of LGBT people now take place every year in many towns and cities around the world. These are known as "Pride" events.

LGBT laws

In the United Kingdom, up until just over 50 years ago, gay men could be sent to prison if they were caught kissing or cuddling another man. Even when the law was changed in 1967, sex between men was only permitted if they were aged 21 or over.

At the time, attitudes towards homosexuality were very different from how they are today. Now a **majority** of people thinks that LGBT people should be treated the same way as heterosexual people. Back then, a lot of people thought that relationships between people of the same gender were wrong. This attitude is known as **homophobia.**

Keeping quiet

The fear of homophobic abuse has led many gay and lesbian people to hide their true feelings. Some kept their relationships with other men or women secret, including some famous people.

Sir Ian McKellen, who starred in the *Lord of the Rings* and *X-Men* films, announced that he was gay more than 25 years into his acting career. McKellen made the move so that he could campaign for equal rights for fellow LGBT people.

Sir Ian McKellen

Fast Fact: Homophobia

When homosexual people are targeted with abuse or treated badly because they love someone of the same gender, this is known as homophobia. In the UK, it is a crime to attack someone with words or actions because they are gay or lesbian. People who carry out homophobic "hate crimes" can be sent to prison.

Religion and LGBT

There are many different branches of Christianity, such as Roman Catholicism, Methodism and Anglicanism (the Church of England). Each of these Christian churches have their own view on homosexuality.

In 1976, the Episcopal Church, which began in the United States, became one of the first branches of Christianity to welcome LGBT people. Now members of the Episcopal Church march at events in support of the LGBT community.

Changing beliefs

Many Christians welcome LGBT people into the church. Some churches allow lesbians and gay men to become vicars and priests. The Muslim Council of Great Britain believes that most British Muslims have a laid-back approach to LGBT people, and gay and lesbian people are welcome in most synagogues in the United Kingdom.

However, some religions still teach that homosexuality is wrong. Some Christians say that the Old Testament of the Bible forbids it. Some Islamic leaders, known as Imams, feel that the Quran forbids homosexuality. In Judaism, some rabbis may feel that love between people of the same gender is wrong.

Carys Jones-McNeill

When did you realize that you were attracted to people of the same gender?

I realized in school that I was attracted to girls, but I didn't do anything about this at the time. I just thought it was close friendship.

As an LGBT person, have you felt accepted in church?

Yes. I've been lucky that as a Methodist they have accepted me from the beginning. The Methodist Church has always welcomed me and my partner, and now our children.

Over the years, how have you been treated by fellow churchgoers?

We have always been treated well and fairly by other Methodists.

What are your hopes for future generations of LGBT Christians?

I hope in future that being LGBT becomes more acceptable in all branches of Christianity, not just some Churches.

I am who I am

In the United Kingdom, over 1 million people are happy to say that they are lesbian, gay or bisexual. That's around two per cent of the people who live here. Yet according to experts, the actual number of people who are attracted to members of the same gender could be even higher. Some people are still uncomfortable about revealing their true feelings, or are worried about what their friends or family might say.

Others are simply confused and don't know what to do when they realize they might be lesbian or gay. There are no rules about when these feelings might start to happen and it's not uncommon for people to lock them up inside or try to ignore them.

Some people are happy to show their support of the LGBT community at public events.

Feelings can change

In 2014, former Premier League and international footballer Thomas Hitzlsperger announced that he was gay at the age of 32. He told a newspaper that he only realized that he was more attracted to men than women in his late twenties.

Up until that point, Hitzlsperger had been engaged to his girlfriend for eight years. He said he wanted to make his LGBT status public so that other gay or lesbian sports stars could feel comfortable doing the same.

Anne-Marie

Chart-topping pop singer Anne-Marie has revealed that she is a bisexual woman, but she doesn't see that as a big deal. In a 2018 interview about one of her music releases, she said, "I've never just been attracted to men or women. I just feel like I'm attracted to who I like. I honestly feel everyone is like that."

Telling friends and family

When someone realizes that they might be lesbian, gay or bisexual, it can be difficult to know what to do next. Should they keep their feelings a secret or tell their friends and family?

Some celebrities have waited a long time to reveal their true feelings. Actress Jodie Foster first became famous in the 1980s but didn't come out until 2013, when she was 51 years old.

I was born this way

Most people who "come out" choose to tell their family and closest friends. Celebrities sometimes take a different approach. In 2014, singer Sam Smith used an interview with *The FADER* magazine to explain that the songs on his new album were about his love for another man. He was aged 22 at the time.

REAL-LIFE STORIES

Orla Robinson Wardley

When did you realize you were attracted to women?

Two years ago when I was 14. I'd always known deep down but it took a while for me to understand what these feelings were.

How did your family react when you "came out"?

They were very positive. They haven't treated me differently.

How are you getting on at school?

School was the scariest part of being an LGBT teenager. I told my closest friends first and knew that if they didn't accept me then they weren't my friends. Most people have accepted who I am.

Fast Fact: What is "coming out"?

"Coming out" is the act of telling people that you are an LGBT person. It is a big deal because you may not know how your friends and family will react. In many cases they will be supportive, but this doesn't always happen.

LGBT relationships

Many LGBT people want to spend the rest of their lives with the person they love.

LGBT relationships are just like any other. There is no difference between the love a man has for a man, or a woman for another woman, and the love between a man and a woman.

Whether you love somebody of the same or opposite gender, you might want to spend the rest of your life with the person of your dreams. All relationships, regardless of who is involved, are based on three things: love, friendship and trust.

Shouting from the rooftops
In 2013, World Wrestling Entertainment (WWE) star Darren Young decided to become the first professional wrestler to "come out". In interviews, he explained that he wanted everyone to know how much he loved his boyfriend, Nick Villa. "We're a normal couple; we do things a normal couple does," he told *People* magazine.

Many LGBT and heterosexual relationships can be committed and loving and can last a long time. Actresses Lily Tomlin and Jane Wagner first started dating in 1971. They're still together now, almost 50 years later.

James Benefield and Rich Taylor

How important was it for you to get married to your partner?

James: Very! I don't think getting married is right for all couples. But it's so important to have it as an option and be equal with any heterosexual couple that wants to get married.

What was the best thing about your wedding day?

Rich: It was so full of love and laughter! To have everyone we care about in one place celebrating with us meant the world.

What are your hopes for future generations?

James: I want to live in a country where I don't have to feel self-conscious to walk down the road holding the hand of my partner. We're almost there!

Love and marriage

If you're in a loving, committed relationship, sooner or later your thoughts may turn to marriage. For centuries, heterosexual couples have had the opportunity to become husband and wife.

For years, LGBT people campaigned for the right to get married and have their relationships **legally** recognized. Their tireless efforts to change the law were eventually successful. Today, homosexual couples can either get married or enter into a **civil partnership**.

Today, many same-sex couples choose to get married.

Fast Fact: Marriage and civil partnerships

In 2004, the UK government passed a law allowing gay and lesbian couples to show their **commitment** by entering into a civil partnership. This gave same-sex couples the same rights as heterosexual married couples. In 2013, the government went a step further, changing the law to allow lesbian and gay couples to get married. However, the law still allows vicars and priests to refuse to marry homosexual couples in a church.

Kelly and Rebecca Roskell-Thomas

Which LGBT person has inspired you the most?

Kelly: Comedian and chat show host Ellen Degeneres. I remember the day she "came out". It was at a time when I was coming to terms with my own sexuality and coming out slowly to friends.

What was the best thing about your wedding day?

Rebecca: The best thing about our wedding day was the location. We got married in front of a frozen waterfall in Iceland having watched the Northern Lights the night before.

How important was it for you to get married to your partner?

Kelly: It was extremely important. Being married meant we were able to express our love for one another the same as any couple entering marriage.

LGBT families

Regardless of their sexuality or **gender identity**, some people want to have children. In the past, committed couples of the same gender would not have been legally recognized as parents of children. They would not be allowed to adopt children either. Today, many homosexual couples are choosing to become parents.

Help from science

Traditionally, it takes a man and a woman to create a baby. It is not possible for same-gender couples to do this through natural means, so they need the help of scientists. It is now possible to create human life in a **laboratory**. Scientists create a tiny **embryo**, which is then placed inside a woman so that it can grow into a baby.

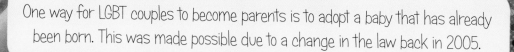

One way for LGBT couples to become parents is to adopt a baby that has already been born. This was made possible due to a change in the law back in 2005.

Lesbian couples who want to become pregnant use **sperm** donated by a man. Gay couples, on the other hand, must find a woman who is not only willing to help create life, but also become pregnant and give birth to their baby. A woman who does this is known as a "**surrogate** mother".

The Drewitt-Barlow Family

In December 1999, Barrie and Tony Drewitt-Barlow had twins, Aspen and Saffron. In doing so, they became the first gay couple in the UK to have children using a surrogate mother and a donated egg. They made the move after their application to adopt a baby was turned down. In the years that followed, Barrie and Tony used the same process to have three more children. Barrie and Tony now help other LGBT couples to become parents at the British Surrogacy Centre they set up in 2011.

Whoever your parents are, what really counts is how much they love you.

Two mums or two dads

When they turned sixteen, Aspen and Saffron Drewitt-Barlow were interviewed on television about growing up with two fathers and no mother. Aspen said, "I don't think they could do any better. A lot of people said they couldn't do it but they've proved everybody wrong."

Some people still think that having two parents of the same gender is strange or "unnatural". They say that it is bad for the children involved. However, 95 per cent of experts say that it makes no difference to how children grow up. These experts point out that having loving parents who care for you deeply is far more important than their gender.

More LGBT families

Today, far more children grow up with same-gender parents than when the Drewitt-Barlow twins were born in 1999. There are also many famous LGBT couples that have children.

Pop singer Sir Elton John and his husband David Furnish have two children, both born to a surrogate mother. In June 2018, Olympic diving star Tom Daley and husband Dustin Lance Black celebrated the birth of their baby son by a surrogate mother in the United States.

REAL-LIFE STORIES

Georgia Barton-Hague

What has it been like growing up with two mothers?

Growing up I never really thought I was much different from anybody else for having two mums because that is all I have ever known.

When you were at school, what was the reaction of your classmates to the fact that you had same-sex parents?

My classmates always had lots of questions. I was asked which mum was my "real mum". I often got frustrated and confused by this question because they were both real mums to me. Some people couldn't accept that and insisted that there had to be only one.

Transgender matters

Being transgender is more about how you feel inside than whether you love people of the same gender.

Body to body

Almost everyone is born with either a male or female body. When you were born, a doctor looked at your body and told your parents that you were a boy or a girl. This is your gender. Most boys and girls grow up happy with who they are, but there are some people who feel like their bodies don't match how they feel inside. These are transgender people.

It can be very confusing growing up with these feelings. In fact, it can take transgender people many years to realize what the feelings mean. They then face a decision about how to live their lives. Some choose to change their names and appearance, telling friends that they are now a girl rather than a boy, or a man rather than a woman.

Doctors and specialists talk at length with their patients about whether gender realignment is suitable for them.

Changing gender

For some transgender people, changing their name and appearance is not enough. They may seek help from doctors to change their bodies to match how they feel inside. This process is called **gender realignment**. This process is usually only done after someone has been living as a transgender person for a number of years.

Gender realignment is complicated and takes time. The first step is hormone treatment. Hormones are chemicals that tell your body whether you are male or female. When a transgender person is injected with the hormone that matches their chosen gender, their body starts to change.

Permanent changes

Some transgender people, such as *Keeping Up With The Kardashians* star Caitlyn Jenner, have operations to change their bodies forever.

Before gender realignment, Caitlyn (pictured right) was a famous former Olympic athlete called Bruce Jenner (left). Bruce lived for years as Caitlyn before having gender realignment surgery.

Difficult times

Not all of those who have "come out" as transgender get a good reception. Transgender sports writer and commentator Philippa York used to be a famous male cyclist called Robert Millar. In 2017, she told the *Daily Telegraph* how difficult it was going outside after her realignment surgery. "I would receive abuse on the street," she said.

Fast Fact: Transphobia

The kind of abuse Philippa was getting is called **transphobia**. Like homophobia or racism, transphobia is against the law. According to research, one third of transgender people in the UK have experienced transphobia at some point in their lives.

Max

When did you first realize that your gender might be different from the female body that you were born in?

From a very young age I wanted to be a boy. I can remember being around four years old and crying all day at my aunt's wedding as they made me wear a dress!

When and how did you first express your new gender identity?

I changed my name at 10 because my parents completely understood that the name they gave me didn't fit. I first properly "came out" as transgender when I was 27.

How did your friends react when you told them you wanted to work towards gender realignment?

My closest friends were extremely supportive. They would send lots of articles about what to do but I wasn't quite there. Just saying, "I am trans" was a huge deal for me at the time.

LGBT around the world

In the United Kingdom and many other countries, LGBT people have the right to live and love as they please. This is not the case everywhere around the world. According to a 2017 report, there are still 72 countries where same-sex relationships are **illegal**.

In some of these countries, the penalties for being gay or lesbian are severe. There are eight countries that punish homosexuality with the death penalty and many more that send LGB men and women to prison. Many of these countries are in Africa, the Middle East and Southeast Asia.

Hiding love

Life for homosexual and bisexual people in these countries can be very difficult. They cannot express their love in public for fear of being **arrested** by the police and put on trial. Even in countries where being LGBT isn't illegal, life can still be difficult due to other laws or widespread homophobia.

These people are marching in protest against anti-LGBT laws that are in place around the world.

Bisi Alimi

In 2004, Bisi Alimi shocked Nigeria by becoming the first Nigerian man to "come out" as gay on national television. Bisi was **disowned** by his family and friends and received **death threats**.

In 2006 the Nigerian government passed new laws that made being homosexual a crime. Bisi was arrested and put in prison. When he was released in 2007, he received more death threats and had to go into hiding. A month later Bisi secretly fled the country and moved to the UK, where he still lives.

Changing times

Over the last 50 years, acceptance of homosexuality and LGBT people around the world has increased dramatically. Although there are still countries with homophobic laws, it is possible that these too will be overturned in the years and decades ahead.

Marvia Malik (left)

A good example of a country undergoing **rapid** change is Pakistan. There, same-sex relationships are illegal, and homophobic or transphobic attacks are not uncommon. However, few homosexual couples are arrested, put on trial or punished. In May 2018 the country's **parliament** passed a law guaranteeing rights for transgender people. The decision came less than two months after former model Marvia Malik became the first transgender woman to read the news on Pakistani television.

Getting married in the morning

A big change in LGBT rights around the world has been the number of countries that now allow same-sex marriages or civil partnerships. Since the Netherlands passed a law allowing homosexual couples to marry in 2001, 25 other nations have followed suit. These include England, Scotland, Wales, Canada, Spain, France, Brazil, Argentina and New Zealand.

The Republic of Ireland, a country that only scrapped laws against homosexuality in 1983, made civil partnerships between same-sex couples legal in 2010. In 2015, the government passed laws allowing homosexual couples to marry, despite protests from the **Catholic Church.**

In 2015 – the first full year in which marriage became available for same-sex couples in Britain – 6,493 same-sex couples were married in England and Wales. A further 9,156 couples converted their civil partnership into marriage.

Glossary

arrested held by the police because they think you have broken the law

bisexual person who is attracted to both men and women

Catholic Church branch of Christianity that represents Roman Catholics

civil partnership similar to a marriage, this is a way for couples to commit to spending the rest of their lives together

commitment dedicating yourself to something, such as spending your life with someone

death threat threat to kill someone

disown refuse to have any connection with someone

embryo unborn child at its earliest stage of development. An embryo will grow into a baby.

gay homosexual

gender label given to you based on your sex, for example, boy or girl

gender identity way you feel about the gender you were born with

gender realignment medical process of changing your gender

heterosexual person who is attracted to and has relationships with people of the opposite sex

homophobia fear and hatred of homosexual people

homosexual person who is attracted to and has relationships with people of the same sex

illegal against the law

laboratory room or building where scientists work

legal within the law

lesbian woman who is attracted to and has relationships with other women

majority greater part, or more than half, of something (for example a number of people)

parliament organization that makes a country's laws

rapid very fast

sperm male sex cell

Supreme Court highest court in the land. It is often used to make the final decision on law changes.

surrogate woman who is prepared to help someone by becoming pregnant with, and giving birth to, their baby

transphobia fear and hatred of transgender people

Find out more

Books
LGBT Families (Families Today), H.W. Poole (Mason Crest, 2017)
Understanding Sexuality, Honor Head (Franklin Watts, 2017)
Understanding Transgender, Honor Head (Franklin Watts, 2017)

Websites

National support services:
There are many national support services you can contact for advice or support.

childline.org.uk
Childline's counsellors offer support for children under 19 years old either online or on the phone 24 hours a day, 7 days a week.

itgetsbetter.org
The It Gets Better project is a non-profit organization that aims to connect LGBT youths around the world. Over 60,000 people have shared their It Gets Better story so far.

lgbtyouth.org.uk
LGBT Youth Scotland supports LGBT youths living in Scotland.

themix.org.uk
The Mix is the UK's leading support service for young people. It offers advice about issues such as coming out and mental health.

Local support services:
As well as national services, there are many local support services. Search online to see if there are any in your area. Here are a couple of them:

allsortsyouth.org.uk
Allsorts is a Brighton-based youth project that supports and connects LGBT children and young people. They also offer support sessions for trans and gender-questioning children from the age of 5 years old and up.

theproudtrust.org
The Proud Trust are based in Manchester and run the LGBT centre: the first fully publicly funded "gay centre" in Europe. The website offers advice and support on topics such as coming out, support from friends, stress and keeping safe online.

Note to parents and teachers: the Publishers have made every effort to recommend websites that are from trustworthy sources and that are age-appropriate for the readers of this book. However, due to the changing nature of the internet, we cannot be responsible for content shown on these pages and we recommend that all websites are viewed under the supervision of a responsible adult.

Index